Developing Human Resource Information System

Developing Human Resource Information System

Aahok Kumar Gupta

2025

Daya Publishing House®

A Division of

Astral International Pvt. Ltd.

New Delhi – 110 002

First Published, 2005

Reprinted, 2025

ISBN 978-81-7035-318-8

Published by : **Daya Publishing House®**
A Division of
Astral International Pvt. Ltd.
– ISO 9001:2015 Certified Company –
4736/23, Ansari Road, Darya Ganj
New Delhi-110 002
Ph. 011-43549197, 23278134
E-mail: info@astralint.com
Website: www.astralint.com

Dedicated
With Love
and
Respectful Regards
to
My Parents

ACKNOWLEDGEMENTS

In the completion of this study, I owe profound gratitude to Dr. (Mrs.) Srilatha without whose untiring and earnest efforts it would not have been possible for me to complete this work. She spared her valuable time in the midst of her busy schedule of engagements and academic life to guide me.

My gratitude also goes to my wife who gave me encouragement and support to complete this study. I am beholden to my son who helped me a lot in solving critical problems on computer at various points during the period of project. I am also thankful to all my friends who always helped me in the persuit of my study.

I am indebted to the Chairman, Management and staff of International Tractors Limited for their necessary support.

Ashok Kumar Gupta

Contents

List of Tables

1
INTRODUCTION

Personal records have always been necessary for good personnel administration. As business continue to grow and the administration of personnel becomes more sophisticated and professional. The volume of paper records increases in proportion with the new technologies creating new and vastly different records.

Only sound records management can provide accurate information to organization with the necessary checks and balances in paper work and facilitate the retention of information in a uniform and specified manner. Personnel records represent the accumulation of personnel forms and range from forms completed to job description, interview, selection, recruitment, wage and salary administration, appraise, evaluate, training, leave, transfer, promotion, discipline, retirement and termination. Good forms are created to save time and cost and to retain information in an orderly manner. So the main function of HR specialists is to maintain control over the operations and to keep a record of how effectively the human resources have been utilized

The main functions of a record management program are:

- ✰ Record Creation
- ✰ Record Maintenance
- ✰ Record Disposal and
- ✰ Information Flow

The process of record creation involves the process of storing of data in man or machine in readable form. Record maintenance provides the means for controlling, analyzing, classifying and retrieving active recorded information. Record disposition provides the systematic removal of semi active records from expensive space, and concentrating on protection of active, vital and important records. Information flow helps to pass on the required information or data at appropriate time for further decision.

The company International Tractors Limited is engaged in manufacturing agricultural equipment under the trademark of **SONALIKA**. A small factory was established in seventies at Hoshiarpur in Punjab. The small factory, which produced only fifty machines in the year of establishment, has started producing five thousand units within few years and at present it is producing thirty five thousand units per year.

A new factory equipped with modern machinery has already become operative covering an area of fifteen square meters. So is the staff. At present there are fifteen hundred workers on the pay roll. So keeping a personnel record of all the employees in a uniform system requires a through management skill.

2
COMPANY PROFILE

The company under research International Tractors Limited is engaged in manufacturing tractors and agricultural equipment under the trademark *"SONALIKA"*. The company is in the field of manufacturing Agricultural Machinery for the last 35 years. Due to trouble free and excellent performance, Sonalika products and Trademark "Sonalika" became the household name among the ruralites. This encouraged the company to produce more quality implements, which were very well received and soon captured the Indian market. Today, the farm products of Sonalika have major share in the Indian market and only meager share goes to other brands. It is manufacturing more than 75,000 agriculture machines, which is a record in itself. It is all due to the excellent Quality and Superb performance of the farm Implements produced by the company. In 1995, the companies diversified its activities and started its tractor's wing and have started manufacturing complete Tractors, which have also proved to be an outstanding Success. They developed the first tractor DI - 740 and soon this product caught the fancy of farming community and it has gained such a popularity as has not been achieved by any brand so far that too during short span of a few years. The company is manufacturing tractors conforming to the actual needs of the farming community and not just to produce Tractors and force their sales on the ruralites. Success encourage the company it to develop more models from time to time suitable to the pockets of the farmers and catering to their actual needs. Accordingly 12 models have since been developed and marketed ranging from 25HP to 60 HP. These tractors have created a stir in the tractor market due to their outstanding performance. The dedicated team of workers and engineers are lending their full help to make Sonalika International the No.1 in the entire country, which is its ultimate goal.

A small factory was established in 1967 at Hoshiarpur in Punjab state in North India. The small unit, which produced only fifty machines in the year of establishment, started producing five thousand units within few years and at present it is producing thirty five thousand units per year.

A new factory equipped with modern machinery has already become operative covering an area of fifteen square meters. So is the staff. At present there are two thousand workers on the pay roll. The credit for this success goes to Sh. L.D.Mittal, the soft spoken Chairman under whose leadership the company has flourished and is destined to reach still greater heights and his two sons named Mr. A.S. Mittal and Mr. Deepak Mittal, Managing Director and Joint Managing Director respectively of the company, who have been engineering the activities of the company successfully since inception. In recognition of Services rendered in Tractor Industry, Company's Chairman, Managing Director, and Joint Managing Director were publicly honoured. Sh L.D. Mittal Chairman Sonalika International was given Pride of Country award at the gracious hands of Chaudhary Prem Singh Speaker Delhi Vidhan Sabha. 'Udyog Bhushan' was awarded to Sh. Deepak Mittal Joint Managing Director, Sonalika International and Gold Medal for excellent quality in production of tractors was given to Sh A.S. Mittal Managing Director Sonalika International. These awards have been instituted by "Society of industry and Business achievements" and were given away in the presence of large gathering comprising of Business and Industry magnates of the country as a whole.

International Tractors Limited, the rapidly growing Tractor Company, has also been awarded the ITID Quality Excellence Award, instituted by the institute Of Trade and Industrial Development.

The company has a network of more than 600 dedicated Dealers throughout the length and breadth of India and in Nepal. All of them are fully equipped with Salc and Service infrastructure. In addition company has a team of devoted specialist Engineers and Marketing Executive. Factory is equipped with Ultra Modern Machinery Equipment. At present SONALIKA GROUP have many big and small ancillary units to manufacture different equipments in farming sector.

GROUP COMPANIES

- ☆ International Tractors Limited
- ☆ Sonalika Agriculture Industries
- ☆ Sonalika Capital Limited
- ☆ Punjab Agriculture Industries
- ☆ Casting Corporation of India

PRODUCTS

- ☆ Multicrop Threshers
- ☆ Crop Reapers

- ☆ Potato Planters
- ☆ Maize Sheller (Corn Threshers)
- ☆ Seed cum Fertilizer Drill
- ☆ Paddy Threshers
- ☆ Potato Diggers
- ☆ Harvesting attachments
- ☆ Submersible Pumps.

Different Models of Tractor

- ☆ DI 730
- ☆ DI 730 III
- ☆ DI 732 III
- ☆ DI 35
- ☆ DI 740
- ☆ DI 745 III
- ☆ DI 750
- ☆ DI 750 III
- ☆ DI 55
- ☆ DI 60

MULTY CROP GRAIN-cum-PADDY THRESHER

SONALIKA, The harvest specialists, introduce one more to their credits of threshers the multi crop thresher capable of threshing not just rice but every thing like Wheat, Maize, Sorghum, Sun flower, Ragi, Bhajra all other millets with minimum loss and maximum output and cleaning efficiency. SONALIKA Multi crop thresher consists of crop feeding chute, threshing cylinder, and blower, oscillating winnowing box, straw walker and grain outlet. The rash bars of the threshing cylinder and the chaff separate the grain. Dust and other impurities are winnowed away by blower. The clean grain is collected through the sieves, which are changeable according to the crop to be threshed.

The straw is discharged through ladder like straw walkers available on 7.5 H.P. and 10 H.P. ranges.

DEALER NETWORK

The Company believes in selling and excelling true to its business principles and providing service after sales to create further confidence in the customers. The company has appointed more than 600 dealers spread in the length and breadth of the country covering Punjab, Haryana, Himachal Pradesh, Uttar Pradesh, Madhya Pradesh, Maharastra, Rajasthan, Gujarat, Andhra Pradesh and Orissa. Process for appointing dealers in Karnataka, Tamilnadu and West Bengal is also on the last stage. The company has already appointed some dealers in Nepal. Dealers are a devoted lot who have made their fortunes due to their association with SONALIKA.

SERVICE AFTER SALES: THE TOP PRIORITY

The company has posted 35 qualified Agriculture Engineers at various important centers of the country to take care of after sale service without any time gap to over 70,000 satisfied customers and this number is multiplying day by day. There are some regional centers to attend the complaint without delay.

Engineers are available at Hoshiarpur for Punjab & H.P., for Haryana, Rajasthan, U.P. at Delhi, for Gujarat at Ahmedabad, for Maharashtra at Pune and for Bihar, West Bengal & Nepal at Patna.

Apart from this, the company has opened its own servicing centers to augment process of giving efficient service to the customers at the nearest points. The mechanics of the dealers are being given training at their work place and at Hoshiarpur plant in a phased manner so that they familiarize with the new tractors and repairing and servicing is done more efficiently and scientifically. There is a quick response to the servicing complaints. The review of the servicing complaints/suggestions is daily done at company's Hoshiarpur Plant between 4 to 5 PM under the Chairmanship of Joint M.D. The servicing complaints if any are taken up and remedial action is taken wherever necessary.

INTERACTION WITH TRACTOR USERS

Our Engineers/Marketing's top officials are regularly contacting the Sonalika Tractor users by visiting their villages. As per feed back available the sonalika Tractor owners were surprised to see a Tractor representative visiting their place. This proves amply that visits of Sonalika officials have created a confidence in the farmers and they in turn have wished the company a great success, which in fact is helping the farming community to increase their field-yields through farm implements and a complete and perfect Tractor. Similar exercises to visit the clients at their home place and to enquire about the health of the tractors and exchange pleasantries have been held in other parts of the country. This process is on to build a complete rapport with the farmers.

MAN POWER

There are more than 2000 employees on the pay roll. Each Company is divided into various sections and departments, which are headed by well qualified and experienced Supervisors and Managers.

RESEARCH &DEVELOPMENT

There is continuous stress on Research & Development. Old designs are being improved and new designs are being created by our R & D Staff.

QUALITY CONTROL

Quality control is very strict. Each component has to undergo stringent quality tests. After being tested by the Department there is a system of Audit test also, So that there is no laxity at any level. Moreover after the machines/ Tractors is complete it is put to rigorous field test before dispatch to the dealers.

TRAINING

Regular Training Sessions are being held for Engineers as well as dealers. Comprehensive training manuals have been printed and distributed among the technicians as well as sales force.

PLANT

Half a dozen plants are spread over in an area covered about 50 acres of land. Plants are equipped with Modern Machinery & Equipment. The high quality results are being obtained even from indigenous machines. There are spacious halls to house different sections for specific jobs. The plant is mechanized and has been fully computerized. Chief Minister of Punjab inaugurated new modern computerized state of the art manufacturing plant at Hoshiarpur in July 2000. The cream of the industry assisted by skilled and dedicated workers is manning the different departments. Each tractor, which rolls out of the factory, is subjected to strict quality controls. The company has achieved prestigious ISO 9001 and ISO 14001certification in view of its in house facilities backed by computerized and automatic machines, world class R&D, quality controls, standards, & systems.

The plant is located at Hoshiarpur (Punjab), which is declared backward district. Due to this, State government and Government of India are extending lot of benefits and facilities. Hence company is able to produce high quality products at most competitive rates.

IN SEARCH OF GLOBAL MARKETS

After having done exceedingly well in the domestic market the tractors manufactured by Sonalika are finding their way to global markets also. Export to Sri Lanka, France, Bangladesh, Nepal and African Countries has also started. Shipment to United States and Australian markets are at the final stage.

Collaboration with RENAULT Agriculture

Sonalika has not stopped. It believes in improving upon its performance and accelerating pace of progress further. The Company has signed an MOU with world renowned automobile giant RENAULT Agriculture of France (with annual turn over of US $ 34 billions) on 30/04/99. As per the Agreement RENAULT Agriculture will provide Technical know how, financial assistance and Market support for Export. Some of the accessories of the Tractors like Seed, Cabins and Gears may have to be imported from Italy soon to make the company more modern. The world class technology from World Renowned RENAULT has enabled Sonalika Tractors to give Indian farmers the most modern "State-of-the-Art" tractors at the lowest rates with excellent pulling power, superb design and low consumption of fuel have proved their superiority over others. This collaboration has also helped the company in earning foreign exchange by exporting tractors made in India to foreign land covering Southeast Asia, Africa and Europe.

Collaboration with UK's MG Rover Group Ltd.

The Company has also signed an MOU with UK's world renowned automobile giant MG Rover Group Limited to manufacture a sports utility vehicle and small cars in technical collaboration.

ISO 9001 and ISO 14001 Certifications in Recognition of Quality and Standards

International Tractors Limited with Sonalika brand of tractors have been certified as ISO 9001 which is highest level of certification issued by International Standards Organization which indicates world class research and development, quality control and perfect systems of company that too within short span of its inception.

The scope of registration covers design, development, production and installation. The registration is a quality mark. Sonalika has also been certified as ISO 14001 that is another golden feather in company's cap and another stamp of quality.

Company has developed a tractor engine in 50 HP ranges which conforms to Euro II norms and which incidentally is the first engine in India.

CMERI Government of India Transfers Design and Technology to Sonalika

International Tractors Limited has made rapid strides within a short span of 6 years. It has not only made its presence felt in the Tractor Industry but has made in-roads into the market share of popular brands. Its valued and satisfied customers are multiplying and have crossed 63,000 mark.

This phenomenal growth is the result of hard work coupled with dedication at all levels. On the top of it, company has never compromised on quality. This is precisely the secret of success of the company. Company have been after a world class technology so that Indian farmers get the best value for their hard earned money.

CMERI (Central Mechanical Engineering Research Institute) Government of India, which has many firsts to its credit in many fields, has helped Sonalika a lot in enriching the Company with technological advancements and transferring technology for Sonalika Tractors for all models ranging from 32 HP to 60 HP.

Group Turnover and Projections

Group Turnover as on 2002 are as under:

Year	*Tractors*	*Machinery*
1996-97		
1997-98		
1998-99		
1999-00		
2000-01		
2001-02		

	1996-97	*1997-98*	*1998-99*	*1999-00*	*00-01*	*01-02*
Tractors (Nos.)	396	2770	6211	8773	13496	17002
Agriculture Machinery (Nos.)	5000	7500	12000	18000	24000	32000

Growth in Tractor Sales (Nos.)

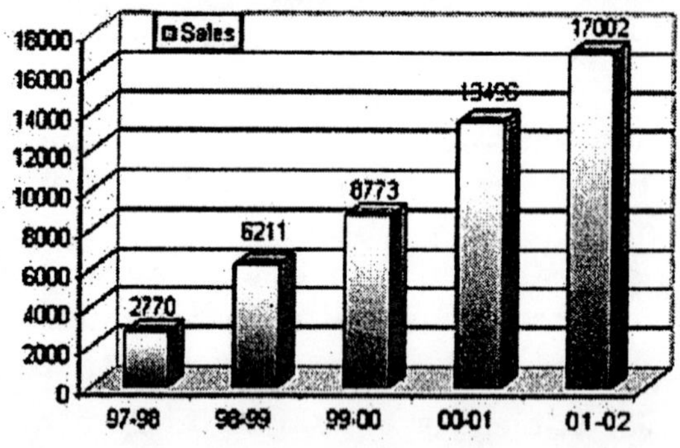

GROWTH PLANS

In future Plans Company has intentions to introduce world class Technology in our Agriculture Implements and for that purpose it is negotiating with some Italian and European Companies for importing the technology components from the European Countries. Production of tractors for example:

1996-97	1526 Units
1997-98	2770 Units
	6211 Units
1999-2000	15000 Units (Target)

The growth of the company is very high as against the industry growth, which is 30-35% approx. With the help of technical know-how of French partner. Sonalika has plans to produce high quality tractors at reasonable rates to cater all types of agricultural needs of the farmers. This will felicitate the company to earn foreign exchange by exporting tractors made in India to foreign land covering Southeast Asia, Africa and Europe.

3
CONCEPTS

Personal records have always been necessary for good personnel administration. As business continue to grow and the administration of personnel becomes more sophisticated and professional. The volume of paper records increases in proportion, with the new technologies creating new and vastly different records.

Only sound records management can provide an organization with the necessary checks and balances in paper work and facilitate the retention of information in a uniform and specified manner. Personnel records represent the accumulation of personnel forms and range from forms completed to job description, interview, selection, recruitment, wage and salary administration, appraise, evaluate, training, leave, transfer, promotion, discipline, retirement and termination. Good forms are created to save time and cost and to retain information in an orderly manner.

The main functions of a good information management program are:

- ✰ Record Creation
- ✰ Record Maintenance
- ✰ Record Disposal and
- ✰ Information flow

The process of record creation involves the process of storing of data in man or machine in readable form. Record maintenance provides the means for controlling, analyzing, classifying and retrieving active recorded information. Record disposition provides the systematic removal of semi active records from expensive space, and concentrating on protection of active, vital and important records. Information flow helps to pass on the required information or data at appropriate time for further decision.

DATA

Data are a set of isolated raw facts, figures, and statistics, unrelated and un-interpreted. Data could be defined as a collection of numbers, letters or symbols that can be processed, maintained or produced by a management information system (MIS).

DATA

↓

PROCESSOR

↓

INFORMATION

INFORMATION

Information is the result or product of processing data. It provides knowledge or intelligence. It contains an element of surprise; reduce uncertainty and helps to take proper action. Information is an occurrence or a set of occurrences that carry messages and when perceived by the recipients via any of the senses, increase their state of knowledge. Information is the behavior - initiating stimuli between sender and the receiver. Data becomes information when it is processed and placed in some context. Information is the "stuff" of paperwork system just as the raw material to finished product. Information is now considered a resource on the level of money, material, men, machines, methods, markets and management.

Flow of information may be vertical, horizontal or circular. Vertical flow may be either from senior level to junior levels (Downwards), or vice versa (Upward). Circular flow of information is very rare.

FORMS

The personal in any organization can not operate even for a single day without the use of forms. Webster defines a form as "a printed or typed document with blank spaces for insertion of required or requested specific information." Good forms are created to save time, space, money and work. They permit the organization to retain necessary information in a uniform way.

Personal records represent the accumulation of personnel forms. These include the forms completed from advertisement to any post, interview, selection, induction, training, transfer, and promotion, till termination or retirement of the employee. These forms are arranged in alphabetically or numerically or in chronological order.

EMPLOYMENT REQUISITION

Requisition for new employees or replacement of employees can be initiated in different ways. Some companies use a simple memorandum while others use printed forms. Sometimes the where manpower is required fill up the form along with salary, grade, position title and brief description of job duties. Sometimes forms contain only background requirement and the job needs to be fulfilled. Sometimes all that is left on personnel to do the needful.

EMPLOYMENT APPLICATION

Next in the recruitment process is the completion of the employment application. This is essential to the screening and interviewing process and provided basic data about the employee, which remains unchanged and serves as a permanent file on the individual's background.

INTERVIEW GUIDES

Successful interviews need to be planned in advance. Once the prospective employee completes the application blank, the interview process comes next. Some companies use guide sheets, which are completed by the interviewer after the interview takes place in order to evaluate the applicant on certain predetermined criteria related with job profile.

HEALTH RECORDS

Health records are important to an organization because they provide crucial information about the physical condition of the company's most valuable asset-the employee. Most companies require pre-employment physical examinations. This form provides for medical personnel to evaluate the candidate's health status in terms of employment.

WAGES AND SALARY

Once the candidate has successfully completed all the procedures and is made a part of the staff, formalities associated with wage and salary administration starts. Different organizations make use of different forms depending on procedures used for wages and salary administration.

JOB DESCRIPTION

A basic component of the wage and salary Programme is the determination of basic rates of pay. Some companies use job evaluation or analysis to determine the content of the job, the experience required, the degree of supervision necessary, etc. This is usually done with the aid of forms.

A variety of forms may be used by an organization, depending upon the level or position to be evaluated e.g. clerical position, technical personnel, supervisory personnel, etc.

PERFORMANCE APPRAISAL

Traditionally, most companies periodically conduct a performance appraisal of each employee. The appraisals are usually made by an immediate supervisor and are used as indicators at the time of salary revision, promotion, training, etc. As with job analysis, a number of forms may be necessary, depending on the level and type of position.

PERSONNEL STATUS CHANGE

Some employees will inevitably change their addresses, telephone number, qualifications, designations or marital status during their employment and such changes must be noted in several places. A multipurpose form may be designed to handle many of these changes.

ATTENDANCE RECORDS

An attendance record are used to compute wages of the employees, determine number of sick days and days for which benefits are to be paid and makes the supervisor and management easier in evaluating an individual's status at the time of salary review.

Other forms may deal with leave transfer, promotion, training induction, etc. Cost Analysis is also done on the basis of these records.

RECORD MAINTENANCE

In the over enthusiasm of introducing records, organizations at times overlook the basic objectives of a record system. The objective should be to supply information when needed. Information in this context means facts useful for managerial decision making in the area of manpower management function. The element of cost must also be borne in mind and a cost benefit analysis must be carried out to determine what records shall be maintained.

It is also desirable to find out once again what information is actually needed by supervisors and managers to ascertain whether the present system actually supplies the required information or not.

A proper filing system must be maintained for the records. Records must be properly classified so that they can be made available when required. The basic methods of arranging records are alphabetically, chronologically and numerically e.g. individual personnel files are most conveniently arranged alphabetically, while papers within file folders can be arranged chronologically. General personnel correspondence, to be made most useful, can be filed according to subject, which may in turn be numerically coded for easy filing and retrieval.

RECORDS DISPOSAL

There is a well-known saying that 'There is nothing permanent except change.' Over the centuries, there has been a general philosophical and intellectual acceptance of the notion that changes in all human system is inevitable and continuous. But in the 20th century, particularly in the last few decades, there has been growing evidence that the pace of change in all walks of life is becoming increasing fast. Organizations that do not change or do not keep pace with the changing environment suffer from entropy and soon become defunct. Change can be defined as an alteration to the existing fields of forces, which tend to affect the equilibrium. So is the case with data and information. Technology innovations have multiplied, products and know-how are fast becoming obsolete, competition has sharply increased, and new ideas are developing vastly. So new data and information is generating at very high speed. It becomes very difficult to store new information in the same limited space. We have to either generate new space or we have to delete or shift the non-active data at some other cheap location to store new one, latest and in use information.

Records pass through 3 stages in their life cycle:

- ☆ Active use
- ☆ Occasional reference
- ☆ Inactive use

Records, which are inactive and are used occasionally as a reference, must be placed in low cost storage area. A record retention schedule can be drawn up keeping in mind statutory and administrative constraints. A periodic review can be built into the system so that forms, records and reports, no longer used are deleted and new ones added.

COMPUTERS IN THE PERSONNEL DEPARTMENT

Throughout the last decade, Organisations have made increasing utilization of computers as a management tool in fulfilling their objectives. Personnel management has recognized the need to obtain more data, more rapidly and in a more accurate form, in order to analyse the information at the earliest to make sound business decisions. In the past the need for such data may have been recognized but because data was scattered throughout the organization, inaccurately maintained or in some cases not available at all. Decisions had to be made in the absence of meaningful information. Thereafter many organizations have recognized this need for timely and accurate information on employees and have developed and implemented personnel data systems in a systematic way.

In industry today, the term personnel data systems normally refer to the mechanized method for the creation and maintenance of data on their employees, the reporting of such data and the subsequent destruction of such data. A personnel data system may encompass all the functional areas within the personnel, or it may be limited to one or two areas such as records and salary and wages data. The utilization of computers within the personnel has usually taken place in the following broad areas:

- ✰ Records and administration,
- ✰ Salary and wages administration
- ✰ Skills inventory and
- ✰ Employment.

Personnel records and administration is the area where the most tangible savings can be realized. It includes such items as keeping track of the status and progress of the employees and basic employee data. Therefore it is not surprising that this is the area in which most computer applications have begun. The main advantages of the application of computers in this area are the savings in clerical time, increased accuracy, imposed standardization and easy to prepare uniform, routine and special reports.

The growth in the use of computers to store of personnel data has increased due to the advantages that such device can make it possible to store and retrieve vast amounts of information about employees, which are so vitally needed to properly exercise the responsibilities of the personnel. Such data is made available at very nominal incremental cost. It also provides for a degree of accuracy that otherwise may not be obtained.

COMMANDAMENTS OF EFFECTIVE RECORDS

It is very important to be clear about the objectives maintenance of the records should be according to the objectives. Following points are very necessary in this regard.

- ☆ Keep records at a minimum, consistent with the requirements of the organization.
- ☆ Be sure that the benefits outweigh the costs of the records decided upon.
- ☆ Easily accessibility of the information when it is needed.
- ☆ Keep the records up to date.
- ☆ Design forms in such a way that they are easy to complete and provide data that can be easily used.
- ☆ Give specific instructions on how the form is to be completed
- ☆ Avoid duplication of entries in different forms.

4

OBJECTIVES OF THE STUDY

The purpose of the study was defined after a review of literature on Human Resources information Systems. The focus of attention on the present study **Developing Human Resource Information System in an Growing Organisation** is non-statutory record systems. As system of storage of information and flow of relevant information at the relevant time is the back bone of any organisation so while completing the project following main objectives of the study are kept in mind:

- ☆ To assess the need for Personnel Records Systems.
- ☆ To design record creation methods.
- ☆ To develop a system for record maintenance and disposal System.

- ☆ To develop a MIS based on personnel information to ensure effective functioning of the personnel.
- ☆ To study the effectiveness of the existing information record systems and suggest modifications.

These objectives were defined and discussed with Chairman-cum-Managing Director and other Officials of the company after discussions with the project guide. This was taken as the researcher's guide as to what is expected from the research.

The nature of the research was defined as conclusive as research findings were expected to result in specific decisions or actions being taken.

5
RESEARCH METHODOLOGY

Research methodology is the plan, structure and strategy of investigation conceived so as to obtain answers to research questions. The case method of study has been adopted to understand the business situation. The case method involves intensive study of a relatively small number of situations. The emphasis is on obtaining a complete description and understanding of the relationships of factors in each instance, regardless of the number involved. The case method is applicable both to secondary and descriptive studies.

This method is of particular value when one is seeking help on a problem in which the interrelationships of a number of factors are involved, and in which it is difficult to understand the individual factors without considering their relationships. Direct observation method is very useful to clear up all the points, which cannot be studied by other method, and also gave him an idea of whole problem and solutions. But the sight of the researcher at the work place may cause some stress and workers may dislike being observed.

The advantages of this method are:

Inferences are obtained from the study of the entire situation, rather than from the study of one or several selected aspects alone.

This is the description of a real event or situation.

More accurate data are obtained, probably as the result of the rapport that is established between the researcher and the respondent and the reduced reliance on formalized questions and answers.

The disadvantages of this system are the lack of objectivity. Since case study involves detailed description of the complete situation, it is very difficult to develop formal methods of observation and recording. Also, since by definition, formal statistical procedures are not used, the analyses are based on the perception of the investigator. So sometimes the results are influenced by the biases of the researches.

CHECKLIST OF INFORMATION REQUIRED

After establishing statement of the study's purpose and objectives, a list of information required to attain the objectives was prepared. As the research was intended to provide information for planning activity, the items for information were defined in somewhat specific terms.

DATA COLLECTION

To achieve the objectives set before, primary and secondary sources of data were studied. Efforts were made to determine whether such information was available in company records and to identify who had the needed information and how it could be obtained.

To interview the concerned personnel specialists, the interview pattern was adopted, as this is very versatile and flexible. The questioning could be adapted to the situation. Further clarification and explanations could be requested if desired.

ANALYSIS OF DATA AND PREPARATION OF PROJECT REPORT

The data obtained through the interviews with personnel Manager and employees was compiled and studied. The existing methods of record creation, record maintenance and disposal were analyzed. The shortcomings of the existing systems were articulated after detailed discussions with personnel Manager.

Existing forms were modified, new forms were designed to overcome the shortcoming in the existing systems and have been covered under recommendations.

Finally the findings of the study were presented in the form of a project report.

INFORMATION NEEDS

Since the dawn of civilization, people have required information to aid them in their personal battle of survival as well as in their attempts to manage their organizations. Through for centuries man lived on earth without keeping records. It became necessary for man to adjust with the growth of social organizations. As tribes grew into nations, trade and commerce developed. Historians have traced some type of record keeping and data processing back to about 3500 BC.

The Babylonian merchants were keeping records on clay tablets. Egyptians made a great improvement and developed papyrus and a sharp pointed pen called a 'calmus'. The world has gone through the agriculture revolution, industrial revolution and now we are in the midst of the so-called "**Information Revolution**".

Existing Systems of Record Creation in Relation to:

- ☆ Recruitment
- ☆ Selection
- ☆ Training
- ☆ Performance Appraisal
- ☆ Attendance, etc.
- ☆ Job Rotation, enlargement and enrichment
- ☆ Promotion
- ☆ Retirement, suspension, termination

Existing System of Record Maintenance

- ☆ Disposal of irrelevant records.
- ☆ Role of computers in the personnel.
- ☆ Other tools that can be employed in effective record creation and management so that the personnel can work more efficiently.

6
EXISTING PERSONNEL INFORMATION RECORD SYSTEMS

RECRUITMENT

The acquisition of employees is a most important and complex task. A company cannot prosper, grow or even survive without adequate human resources. To find and employee the best individuals available is every personnel manager's goal. The manpower plan provides the raw material for the recruitment process.

Recruitment activity begins when the personnel receives a personnel requisition. The request for new personnel is discussed with the concerned department and if validated by the personnel department, is then forwarded to the managing director for his final approval. This is, therefore the management authorization to spend recruitment expenses and add an individual to the payroll, and serves as a communication device between management and the personnel.

The requisitions are sought to be maintained on the basis of that have initiated the process. A master file is created in the central data bank to provide a consolidated account of employee requisitions.

The record of requisitions is disposed off after the personnel takes the required action.

SCREENING AND SELECTION

Selection procedures may vary from one organization to another organization in terms of size, industry, location etc. But the selection process depends upon effective job analyses. The selection process involves the following steps:

- Preliminary Screening of applications
- Review of application forms
- Physical examination
- Checking references
- Psychological Testing
- Interview and
- Internal promotion program.

After getting a sufficient number of qualified applicants from various sources, the next step is the screening and selection of candidates.

The recruitment machinery needs to have detailed information on the nature of the jobs to be filled and the qualities required of the people filling them. This information is recorded in the Job description. This information, as collected by the job analyst, is written in a standard form developed for the organization. This will result in the articulation of the desired qualities in a candidate.

CURRICULUM VITAE

Curriculum vitae are often the tool used to decide whether to interview an advertising response, and employment agency referral, or a write in candidate. This is normally a subjective narrative description of an individual's education, experience and personal information.

APPLICATION BLANKS

An application blank is used so that the company can gain information in a structured and factual manner. Different forms are used for the managerial and non-managerial category workers. These forms have been designed in relation to the company's business and job requirements. They are designed to be easy to read, concise, clear and well spaced.

Principal information requested in application blanks includes name, address, telephone number, health and physical handicaps, education, job history, etc. Similar questions are grouped together and conclude with the signed statement that the information given in application is correct and the individual understands that he is subject to discharge for any wrong statement found any time in future.

If the applicant is selected, this application is filed in his personal file. The application blanks or curriculum vitae of rejected candidates are placed in a data bank. This consists of files that are maintained according to the qualifications of the applicants e.g. Graduates, Diploma Holders, etc.

MEDICAL RECORD

This is usually the last step in the employment process. The main reason for this is to determine, if the applicant qualifies for the physical requirements of the position, to take into account any medical limitations that should be taken into account in the placement of the applicant, to establish a record of the applicant's health at the time of joining, to reduce absenteeism and turnover. The employee is required to get the certificate by a registered medical practitioner.

PERSONAL FILE

Basic personal records are needed for each employee for a number of purposes. So a personal file of every employee is maintained. This file contains:

- ☆ Filled-in Application Blank
- ☆ Bio-Data (if any)
- ☆ Medical examination form
- ☆ Copies of Education Certificates
- ☆ Leaving Report (from previous employer)
- ☆ Joining Report
- ☆ Declaration
- ☆ Copy of the appointment letter

This also contains further details of the employment history of the individual. This includes information on transfers, promotions, increments and details of appraisals.

On leaving, the relieving order is placed in the file. A copy of the no dues is also placed in this file. Then the file is closed. Closed files are maintained as long as space permits.

TRAINING

Training is a significant management tool in bringing about change. For this, it must be systematic and orderly in providing assistance to solve organizational problem and to meet the organization goals.

All fresh employees are inducted into the organization with a formal induction programme, which introduces them to the organization and its working.

In order to update the knowledge and skills of employees at SONALIKA, need-based training and development programs are organized for employees at each level. The training needs of the employees are highlighted in the annual performance appraisal. These needs are then evaluated by the personnel and discussed with the individual employee.

Training programs are conducted with the help of internal expert faculty as well as by external agencies. The employees with individual training needs are sponsored for specialized training to reputed institutes in the country.

Training from external sources is being noted in the personal record if a certificate is produced and a copy of this is placed in the personal file.

WAGES AND SALARY ADMINISTRATION

When new employee joins the organization, the personnel department passes on this information to the accounts department, as the payroll function is discharged by the accounts. A copy of the appointment letter is sent to the time office and to the accounts department

After the joining of a new employee in the organization, an intimation slip is sent to the security, time office and the accounts so that they can make the necessary additions in their records.

It is the responsibility of the personnel dept for maintaining a record of the number of days worked in month. The time office provide this information and this input is used by the accounts department in calculating salary. Other information such as medical bills, etc., is also sent to the accounts to enable them to take the necessary action.

ATTENDANCE SYSTEM

Managerial level employees are required to sign in their attendance in a register maintained at the gate. Staff employees use a punch card to register their attendance. A daily record of attendance is prepared at the time office.

A daily report of attendance is prepared which is forwarded to the Manager (Administration). A copy of the weekly attendance report is sent to Director in charge his perusal. A monthly report that provides details of days worked by the employees is also prepared and sent to Managing Director.

A copy of this report is sent to the accounts so that then can make the payroll according to these details.

LEAVE SYSTEM

An employee at SONALIKA is entitled to avail 10 days casual leave in one calendar year. Un availed part of the casual leave in a calendar year can be availed in the first three months of the next calendar year.

An employee is also entitled to 10 days of sick leave in a calendar year. A medical certificate is required if the leave is more than two days.

An employee is entitled to 30 days of earned leave on full pay for each completed year of service. An advance notice of 7 days is required if the leave applied for less than 7 days. An advance notice of 15 days is required if the leave applied for is more than 7 days.

An individual applying for leave fills in the number of days of unapplied leave due to the employee. The section head is the final approving authority. This sanctioned leave is forwarded to the time office that makes a note in the daily attendance register.

PERFORMANCE APPRAISAL

SONALIKA has a formal performance appraisal system that is used as a tool for employee development and growth. It helps evaluate the potential of an employee based on which the necessary inputs are provided for the development of the individual. Thus the aim of the appraisal system is to improve performance, to assist the development of talents and to identify individuals who have high potential.

As an appraiser, one should make a proper action plan that records every activity of the appraise. This action plan includes remedial action, tips on improving particular aspects of performance, which are not up to the mark. As part of developmental action, appraiser has to reinforce personal strengths and provide guidance and training for acquiring new skill to cope with future work challenges.

Before starting appraisal performance proper homework by appraiser is also very useful. This homework should focus on appreciation and for appreciation find the evidences in the past. A periodic record keeping can be useful. The appraiser can preview the records and entire period instead of immediate past.

Keeping in view, the above a standard form was designed which lists the significant factors considered denoting effective performance. Factor headings are subdivided and against each are a series of rating factors, which range from Performance exceptionally higher than the requirements of the job to Performance needs improvement to meet the requirements of the job. In addition, the appraisal form requires assessment in narrative form discussing reason, data and incident supporting the rating.

This form is filled in by the employee's immediate superior, following guidelines set by HRD and is finalized by the Department head. An appraisal discussion is held with the appraise and follow up actions such as job rotation, transfer training are highlighted.

A record of the employee performance is maintained in his personal file and forms the basis for personnel actions such as grant of increments, training inputs, promotion, transfers etc.

SHORTCOMINGS OF THE EXISTING PERSONNEL RECORD SYSTEMS

There is no standard form available to inform the personnel about need for personnel. This information is communicated though memos and letters to the personnel.

The curriculum vitae of candidates desirous of employment in SONALIKA are voluminous and are maintained according to their qualifications in various files. These forms are arranged chronologically according to the date of applicants. Forms of candidates who are found unfit by the organization are also maintained in the same files and this forms a consolidated data bank. However, it is very difficult to access relevant information from these files hence there is need to develop alternate systems of storage of information.

There exists no means of ensuring that the personnel have imparted all the information that is required by a new inductee. There is also no means of judging the efficacy of the induction programmes for the new inductee.

The training need of the employee is highlighted by the annual performance appraisal. However there in no means for the personnel to capture information needed by it to tackle the training needs of individuals that are highlighted during other periods. A standard form to capture such data would go long way to help the personnel to consolidate this data and to take action subsequently on these training needs.

The personnel do not have any means to evaluate participant reaction to the various training programs conducted by it to tackle the training needs of individuals. This is an important means to judge the effectiveness of the training programmes.

However the Personnel Department maintains personal records of employees, but there is no consolidation of information available in the personnel files of the individual. Hence it is difficult to trace the employment history of the individual in the organization-including valuable information on positions held, salary increases, training programs attended. Consolidation of such information would go a long way in improving the personnel s ability to quickly access such information and to make effective decisions regarding employee placement, transfers, career development, etc.

There is no means available to elicit employee suggestions about improvements in their work. An employee suggestion scheme can go a long way in enabling the organization to incorporate valuable suggestions for improvement in the work situation. Employee participation is required to be encouraged.

The personnel is required to send certain information to the corporate office at the end of every month. The information heads are specified. However there is no standard way of presentation of this information in a clear and standard manner.

7
RECOMMENDATIONS

The following recommendations were suggested.

RECRUITMENT

Personnel requisitions are communicated to the personnel department through memos, etc. there is need to have a standardized Personnel Requisition Form that provides the personnel with the required information it needs in order to commence the recruitment and selection process. The is identified on the form, as well as the position title and a brief description of job duties. It also contains background requirements such as education and experience and the date the job needs to be filled. If the requisition has been generated to replace an employee currently on the payroll, the provides for reasons for termination of employee.

An integrated computer based record of applicants can be maintained to tackle the vast number of applications that are received. This can deal with some basic information heads and be coded according to the qualification of the applicants. On the basis of information collected through the study of Memos, personnel requisition form was designed as following:

Table 1

SONALIKA PERSONNEL REQUISITION FORM

Date:

Requisition No.:

Department/Office:

Location:

(A) Job Title

(B) Work Location

(C) Date needed

(D) Employment Status

- ✰ Regular
- ✰ Casual
- ✰ Vocational Trainee
- ✰ Other (Please specify)

(E) Job Requirements

(F) Brief description of duties:

(G) Qualification required

(H) Experience

(I) Increase to the staff?

Yes/No

(J) (Please give comments)

(K) Replacement for: JobTitle:

Grade:

Promoted

Transferred

Resigned/
Terminated

Others

(L) Approvals

(M) Personnel 's Comments

(Designation/Date)

SELECTION

The interview is at the central point of the employment process. It is therefore the most important means by which an employer secures the information necessary to describe an applicant accurately, in reference to the requirements of a position. It also enables him to make accurate statements of a situation, and about the employee's probable performance in a position.

To serve as a guide in this process and to enable a comparative assessment of candidates, a interview guide sheet can be utilized. This details the required qualifications and experience requirements. This helps the interview panel in assessing the candidate. Interview evaluation sheet was designed to select the best candidates easily.

Table 2

SONALIKA INTERVIEW EVALUATION SHEET

POSITION

DATE

Please complete the form and return to the personnel Deptt.

Characteristics:

Above

Below

Exceptional

Average

Education:

Experience:

Other job related skills:

Expression:

Growth potential:

Sales ability:
(where applicable)

Salary Package:

Willingness to travel:

Willingnes to relocate:

Additional comments:

Major shortcomings:

Interviewer's recommendations:

Employ

Consider

Refer to another

Reject

Interviewer's signature and designation:

Date:

To ensure that the induction process of new employees is carried out properly, an induction checklist has been drawn up. This indicates the items to be covered by the personnel so the new inductee is provided with the necessary information about the company, about his, about his job and that the necessary paperwork is completed.

Table 3
CHECKLIST FOR PERSONNEL DEPARTMENT

1st Day in the office

- ☆ Presentation on Company
- ☆ Induction manual
- ☆ Appointment Approval form
- ☆ File Application (Employment Form)
- ☆ Joining Report
- ☆ Declaration
- ☆ Medical Form
- ☆ Salary Details
- ☆ P.F. norms
- ☆ Insurance norms
- ☆ Photo for ID
- ☆ Explanation of Formats used
- ☆ Office timings
- ☆ Lunch timings
- ☆ Leave system
- ☆ Salary system
- ☆ Other Welfare provisions
- ☆ Introduction to HOD's; Executives, Staff of other s
- ☆ Knowledge about Functions, Systems, Procedures, in the organization and its relationship.
- ☆ Other activities in the organization in brief.

2nd Day in the office

Exlanation about the Department in which he or she is supposed to work. Organization and its relationship to other activities in the organization in detail.

Explain the following

Employee's job role

- ☆ Duties
- ☆ Standards
- ☆ Discipline
- ☆ Housekeeping

Explain Organization standards.

- ☆ Performance of duties
- ☆ Attendance & punctuality
- ☆ Handling confidential information
- ☆ Explain Appraisal system
- ☆ Explain Department, training procedures
- ☆ Introduction to HOD fellow workers (interaction) and
- ☆ Date of follow up interview

EVALUATION FORMS

To evaluate the existing systems various evaluation forms has been designed so that the effectiveness of the induction Programme may be evaluated. This will enable the company to take required steps to overcome the shortcomings in the existing program. An Induction program evaluation form has been prepared.

INDUCTION PROGRAMME EVALUATION FORM

We hope that induction was a rewarding experience for you at SONALIKA; we invite your comments and suggestions about the programe so that we can improve the system to make it more meaningful for new inductees.

- ☆ Did you receive required guidance and assistance in completing paper formalities?
- ☆ Were the rules, regulations and policies properly explained to you or not?
- ☆ What additions can be made in the orientation manual to make it more meaningful for new inductees?
- ☆ Are you satisfied with the inputs and assistance provided by other s during your orientation meetings with them (i.e. reception, time devoted, flow of information, etc.)?
- ☆ Do you have any suggestions for improvement in the above section of the orientation programme?
- ☆ Did you get enough information about the organization and its working? Please explain your answer.
- ☆ Which section of the orientation programme was most meaningful for you? Please explain.
- ☆ To what extent were you involved in you orientation programme
    - ☆ Deeply involved
    - ☆ Interested
    - ☆ Slightly involved
    - ☆ Not much interest
- ☆ Please explain your answer with remarks:
    - ☆ What are your expectations from?

- ☆ Your job
- ☆ Your company

(For those employees who have undergone training) What suggestions would you have for improving the training programme?

(Signature/Department.)

However, the training needs of the employees are highlighted in the annual performance appraisal, but there is need to tackle the training needs that arise in the intervening period. A training need assessment form has been designed so that the personnel can take note of the training needs of employees and design training programs to tackle these.

Table 4
SONALIKA TRAINING NEED ASSESSMENT FORM

Department/Office:

Location:

Name of Employee:

Designation:

Job Description

TRAINING NEED:	Authority imparting Training	Time Period
Job Knowledge	In house	Urgent
Orgn. Knowledge	External	Within 3 Months
Interpersonal Skill	(PL.Explain Agency	Within 6 Months
Written Communication		Within 01 Year
Use of Computers		
Decision Making		
Others (PleaseExplain)		

Signature of HOD

Dy. Manager (P&A)

Trainning programs for managerial and non-managerial cadre employees are envisaged. How participants respond to training programme is important in influencing its effectiveness. To evaluate participant's reactions, training evaluation form has been designed. This will be useful in assessing what has taken place and provide useful feedback to improve training programs.

Table 5
SONALIKA TRAINING EVALUATION FORM

Programme:

Date:

We would appreciate your sharing with us your feelings and reactions to this programme so that we can evaluate it and where appropriate, make changes to improve its usefulness. Please answer the questions below as frankly as possible and use the comments space provided for any additional thoughts or suggestions you may have.

Overall, how would you rate this programme in terms of its value to you? (Please circle one number reflecting your feeling.)

1. Very Very Poor
2. Very Poor
3. Poor
4. Not Bad
5. Fair
6. Average
7. Good
8. Very Good
9. Excellent

For each of the items below, please rate following the rating scale given above:

- ☆ How well was the programme content organized?
- ☆ How well was the material presented by the instructor?

- ☆ How well did the instructor keep your interest?
- ☆ How well did the instructor respond to questions or issues raised by the participants?

COMMENTS

Please rate the various techniques or methods used during the programme in terms of how helpful they were.

- ☆ Lectures
- ☆ Reading material
- ☆ Assignments
- ☆ Class discussion
- ☆ Small group activity
- ☆ Role-playing
- ☆ Cases

In what way could the programme be improved?

PERSONAL FILE

There is no consolidation of information available in the personal file. To overcome this problem and to present a bird's eye view of the contents of the personal file of the employees, a skills Employee Inventory form or card has been devised.

Table 6
SONALIKA EMPLOYEE INVENTORY CARD

- ☆ Name:
- ☆ Address:
- ☆ Designation on joining:
- ☆ Date of birth:
- ☆ Age:
- ☆ Date of joining:
- ☆ Retirement:

- ☆ Marital status:
- ☆ Number of dependants:
- ☆ Education:
- ☆ Previous employment:
- ☆ Employment history in sonalika:

Promotion:

Date w.e.f.:

Location:

Transfer:

Date w.e.f.:

Location:

APPRAISALS:

Date:

By:

Result:

Record Of Salary Revisions:

Date:

Previous Salary:

Revised Salary:

Training Programmes Attended (If any).....

It is also recommended that the files be arranged alphabetically, while papers within these are stored chronologically.

SUGGESTIONS BY EMPLOYEES

A form has been designed to elicit employee suggestions about improvements in the company, division, or employee's job. This will help in implementing a proper and adequate suggestion scheme so that valuable suggestions of the employees can be incorporated in the organization's policies and procedures. The company can get better results with the employee's collaboration and active involvement in the organization's activities.

Table 7
EMPLOYEES' SUGGESTION DATA BANK

Suggestions are particularly welcome on the following subjects:

- ☆ Improvement in service to the customer
- ☆ Improvement in working conditions and reduction of fatigue
- ☆ Improvement in operating methods
- ☆ Savings of material labour or supplies
- ☆ Prevention of waste of every kind
- ☆ Reduction of defective work
- ☆ Elimination of unnecessary records, data, material and equipment.
- ☆ Improved methods of maintaining company property

I suggest the following on this topic or issue:

If further space is required use plain paper or use space on the back of this form.

If other sheets are used show number here_____

Name:

Location:

Your rights on the suggestion become property of the company.

Table 8
SONALIKA MIS
(MANAGEMENT INFORMATION SYSTEM)

The personnel is require to send certain information to the corporate office, at the end of every month. Although Information heads has been specified but there is no standard way of presentation of information on a clear and standard manner. A form called M.I.S. (Management Information System) has been designed to take care of these information needs.

MIS FOR THE MONTH ENDING ____________

(A) Current Manpower

Location:

Staff:

Total Strength:

(B) Additional Manpower Requirements

Qualifications	Employment Status
Vocational Trainee and Grade	Regular
	Date on which Needed

(Annexure: Details of Manpower Qualification/Designation)

(C) Transfer

Sr. No.	Name	Previous Designation	Location Remu.	Present Designation	Location Remu.	Rolls/ status

(D) Promotion

Sr. No.	Name	Previous Designation	Location Remu.	Present Designation	Location Remu.

(E) Training Programmes held/identified

Sr. No.	Name	Location	Duration	No. of Trainees	Teaching Content

(F) Misc. Information

Termination

Suspenstion

Signature

DY. Manager (P & A)

DATA BANK

There is a need of a central data bank that holds the details of employee records and skills inventory and other related information. Skills inventory systems can provide an objective means of selection and placement of employees, thereby utilizing in-house talents to the maximum. For the purpose of data creation, the forms that have been described can provide the input data. The following information can be stored in the data bank:

- ☆ Employee name
- ☆ Number or code
- ☆ Location code
- ☆ Job Classification
- ☆ Salary particulars
- ☆ Employee status
- ☆ Records of transfers and promotions
- ☆ Date of joining
- ☆ P.F./E.S.I. number
- ☆ Date of Birth
- ☆ Age
- ☆ Address
- ☆ Educational Status
- ☆ Martial Status
- ☆ Other job related skills
- ☆ Appraisal ratings
- ☆ Training inputs

Thus a range of output reports can be prepared with this database. These include all basic information about each employee, background history, skills inventory, selection and placement, manpower utilization and planning, personnel statistics and socio-economic, political and religious background etc. This data is utilized whenever there is a need to identify employees for consideration for special projects, additional training, or higher-level jobs. For this purpose, software already available in the market can also be used.

Table 9
JOB ANALYSIS QUESTIONNAIRE

Suggested Position Title:

Supervisor:

Title:

Primary Function of Position:

Principal Duties:

Experience required:

Educational requirements:

Type of supervision (*i.e.* close, general, works independently, etc.):

Number of employees and Job area supervised:

Decisions and Judgments required:

Submitted by:

Name:

Title:

Date:

Table 10
SONALIKA PERSONNEL REQUISITION FORM

Date : Requisition No.

Department/Office Location

(A) Job Title

Work Location Date needed

(B) Employment Status:

- ✰ Regular
- ✰ Casual
- ✰ Vocational Trainee
- ✰ Other (Please specify)

(C) Job Requirements

Brief description of duties:

Qualification required:

Experience:

(D) Increase to the staff? Yes No

(If yes, please give reasons)

Replacement for:	Name	Job Title
Grade:	Reason	Promoted
		Transferred
		Resigned
		Others

(E) Personnel 's Comments

(F) Approvals

Signature

(Designation/Date)

Table 11
SONALIKA INTERVIEW EVALUATION SHEET

Applicant:

Position:

Please complete the form and return
to the personnel Deptt.

Characteristics	Exceptional	Above Average	Average	Below Average
Education				
Experience				
Other job related Skills				
Expression				
Growth potential				
Sales ability (Where applicable)				

Willingness to travel:

Willingness to relocate:

Additional comments:

Major shortcomings:

Interviewer's shortcoming:

Employee

Consider

Refer to another

Reject

Interviewer's signature and designation

Table 12
SONALIKA EMPLOYMENT FORM

Position Applied for : _______

Date

Personal Information

Name

Date of Birth

Occupation

Yearly Income

Address: Present

Address: Permanent

Marital Status

Spouse's occupation

If you belong to SC/ST/OBC

Languages Known
(Tick the Appropriate) Speak Read Write

Medical Information

Blood Group

Doctor
(Name, address & Tel.

Person to be contacted in case
of Emergency

Particular illness or allergic

Educational Qualifications

Degree/ Examination/ Diploma	Year of Passing	Institution/ University	Percentage of Marks taken	Subjects obtained

Any Scholarship/Special awards

Membership of any
Professional or Technical
Institution

Any Special Course
Or Training Undertaken

General Information

Have you ever
Had an interview
With SONALIKA previously?
If so give details
Have you ever been in
Service of SONALIKA before?
If yes, give details
Do you have any relative now Serving in SONALIKA?
If so, give details
Have you ever had any serious
Ailment or handicap ?
If so, state the nature
Did you participate in
Any game or sport? If so,
Give name and level
Of participation.
Describe your hobbies
and interests

Experience

Name and address of employer

(Give most recent employment first)	Period of employment	Basic wage	Total Income

From to At start
When leaving
Other perks
Total Income

Reasons for
Leaving Job

Reasons for
Leaving Job

Reasons for
Leaving Job

MISCELLANEOUS

Do you read regularly

Newspaper Fiction Trade/Technical Journals Magazines

Most interesting subjects

Why ?

Were you awarded for any meritorious
work during service?

State the nature of work you were doing at present

Where you ever involved in any Criminal case

If so, attach complete details

Do you have any objection in our making reference to your present employers

Give two references other than relatives?

Alongwith telephone nos.

1.

2

Answer briefly. Summarize you present
job responsibilities.

How do you consider yourself competent
for this post?

What is your Ambition in life?

Have you entered into any contractual obligation with your present employer

If so, give details.

Any other information you consider relevant?

How much salary do you expect?

If selected when can you report for duty?

DECLARATION

If employed I agree to abide by and observe all rules and regulations of the company that may exist from time. I also agree to assign to the company the entire right, title and interest in and to any invention that I may make relating to company products and methods of manufacturing during employment. I am willing to work on shifts and also agreeable to transfers made by the company. I am willing to work on shifts and also agreeable to transfers made by the company. I am willing to take medical examination when required. I also understand that any misrepresentation of facts on this application will be

Date

Signatures

FOR OFFICE USE ONLY

Employed________________________________

Yes ________________ No. ________________

If yes, then________________Unit__________

____

Joining Date______________________________

Starting Salary____________________________

Remarks

Signatures of Appointing Authority

Sonalika

Address

____

Table 13
SONALIKA APPLICATION FOR EMPLOYMENT (NON- MANAGEMENT)

Post Applied for ....

1. Name (Block Letters)
2. Date of Birth/Age
3. Father's Name
4. Address

   Permanent

   Present (for correspondence)

   Tel. ....

1. Qualifications:

Degree/ Examination/ Diploma	Year of Passing	Institution/ University	Percentage of Marks taken	Subjects obtained

6. Experience:

(Give most recent employment first)	Period of employment		Basic wage	Total Income
	From	To		

7. Do you belong to SC/ST/OBC?

8. Do you have any physical handicap?

9. Salary Expected:
10. Joining time required:
11. Do you have any objection in our making reference to your present employer? Yes/No

12. References (other than relatives):

Name Occupation Address

1.

2

Date

Signature

DECLARATION

If employed I agree to abide by and observe all rules and regulations of the company that may exist from time. I also agree to assign to the company the entire right, title and interest in and to any invention that I may make relating to company products and methods of manufacturing during employment. I am willing to work on shifts and also agreeable to transfers made by the company. I am willing to take medical examination when required. I also understand that any misrepresentation of facts on this application will be

Date Signatures

FOR OFFICE USE ONLY

Employed____

Yes ______________________ No. ____________________

If yes, then______________________Unit_____________

____

Joining Date______________________________________

Starting Salary____________________________________

Remarks

Signatures of Appointing Authority

Sonalika

Address

Table 14
SONALIKA JOINING REPORT

Date:

The Managing Director,
International Tractors Limited.
SONALIKA House,
283, AGCR Enclave,
Karkardooma,
NEW DELHI - 110092

Sub.: Joining Report

Ref.: Appointment Letter No. ______________
Dated: ________________

Sir,

As per my appointment letter referred above, I hereby report for duty in
SONALIKA w.e.f. today the _________________.

Documents attached:

1. Duplicate copy of the appointment letter accepted
2. Copies of Certificates/Testimonials
3. Medical Fitness Certificate

4. Relieving & Service Certificate from the previous employer, if any.

Yours faithfully,

(Signature)

Received the above documents.

Signatures

(Name & Designation)

Dy. Manager (P. & Admn.)

Copy to: Accounts

(Copy of appointment letter enclosed).

DECLARATION

I,________________W/o,D/o,S/o Sh.________________

Resident of____

Solemnly affirm and declare: -

1. That I am married/Un-married/have only one spouse living.
2. That I have never been convicted by any court of law for any offence.
3. That I am not a dismissed employee of any Government/Undertaking/any public or private organization.

4. That I owe my allegiance to the constitution of India.
5. That I shall abide all the rules and regulations applicable in the company from time to time.
6. That I am not directly or indirectly related to any director of the company.

Signature

Date:

Place:

Verification:

I, the above signatory, verify that no part of the above declaration is false and that nothing has been concealed. In case any part of this declaration is discovered at any stage to be false, I shall be liable to be dismissed from the service of the company apart from legal proceedings against me under civil/criminal laws.

Signature

Date:

Table 15
SONALIKA MEDICAL EXAMINATION FORM

1. Name______________________________
2. Father's Husband's Name________________
3. Date of Birth_________________________
4. Height:____________Weight:____________
5. Chest
   (a) Normal_________(b) Expanded_________
6. Vision without glasses
   (R/E)_____________(L/E) ______________
7. Vision with glasses
   (R/E)_____________(L/E)______________
8. Blood pressure & blood group
9. Weight
10. Identification Mark
11. Any other Remark (s)
12. Physical defects, if any
13. Final Report of the Authorized Medical Attendant:

Date:

(Signature)

Name (Dr.)

Complete Address & Tel. No.__________________

PERFORMANCE APPRAISAL SYSTEM-GUIDELINES

OBJECTIVES OF APPRAISAL

- We aim to achieve the following objectives from Performance Appraisal:
- Improve performance by overcoming the weaknesses & building over the strengths.
- Contribute to training, growth & development of the employees.
- Assess the individual's performance with regard to Team, Department & Organizational effectiveness.
- Helpful feedback, guidance, counseling & motivation from the superiors to subordinates - improves relationships.
- Creating a Developmental culture.
- Providing inputs to system of rewards - increments, appreciation, additional responsibility, promotion etc.

USES OF APPRAISAL

The Appraisal form may be used for:

- Clarifying the objectives and the job assignment to your subordinates so that performance appraisal can be done as per objectives set and their accomplishment.
- Identifying weaknesses/improvement areas and finding ways to reduces and overcome the same.
- Identifying training needs for improving your subordinates present performance and future development.

- ☆ Planning for your subordinate's future tasks/ responsibilities, promotion increments, job enrichments etc.
- ☆ Planning a joint action plan for improvement through mutual objective setting.

COMMON ERRORS

- ☆ Be amide of the Road walker.
- ☆ Be unduly harsh or lenient.
- ☆ Get affected by one particular quality.
- ☆ Rate an individual on the basis of group performance.
- ☆ Form preconceived ideas and predict employee performance.
- ☆ Get carried away by regency of good or bad events.
- ☆ Compare employee with your won skills.
- ☆ Take into account circumstantial and situational constraints.
- ☆ Get prejudiced by sex, religion, community and relationship.
- ☆ Get biased by over all image of the employee.

IMPORTANT POINTS

OVERALL APPRAISAL OF AN INDIVIDUAL

The overall appraisal should be based on the following three main planks:

- ☆ Job performance
- ☆ Personal traits/skills
- ☆ Growth potential
- ☆ Inner Hidden Capacities

A 'Star Performer' would score high rating in all the three above-mentioned planks. A good job performer may not be promoted unless he has a good rating in the other two planks i.e. Personal traits/skills and growth potential.

INDIVIDUAL STRENGTH & WEAKNESSES

Good career development for a high performer does not mean that his appraisal should comprise of only A's and B's. Even a good performer can have a weakness in certain factors and that will attract rating "D".

RATING KEY

Normally, the appraiser misinterprets the rating key. To ensure a proper and objective appraisal please read and refer to the explanation of rating key on the top of the appraisal form.

JOB DESCRIPTION

Job description should briefly outline the tasks, activities, responsibilities etc. of your subordinates. Conduct the appraisal in accordance to this job description. Start the appraisal discussion with the job description to avoid ambiguity and misunderstanding of any type.

APPRAISAL DIARY

A good appraiser should maintain an Appraisal Diary. He should record very good and bad incident of performance during the concerned appraisal period. This will ensure an objective appraisal with appropriate ratings on the basis of narration giving proper data, examples and incidents. This will help you in conducting a successful Appraisal Discussion with your subordinate. Since rating will be backed by a proper narration and have a better chance of carrying conviction with your subordinate.

DEFINITIONS OF FACTORS

For uniform and proper appraisal, brief definition of each factor has been given. Both, the appraiser and appraise should follow this definition instead of their own interpretation of any factor.

NARRATIVE ASSESSMENT

The narrative assessment is very important, as it will ensure proper thinking, review of specific incidents, examples and data before arriving at a rating. This will prevent a situation whereby you may give fast and whimsical judgment rating. Moreover this helps in conviction of the subordinate by justifying the rating with a few words & narration. The success of an Appraisal Discussion depends on the narration which is communicated to the appraise. From the Narrative Assessment, specific training needs emerge which can be taken up as a follow up action. Lastly, this can be a useful record in the personal file of your subordinate.

CUSTOMER ORIENTATION

There is a urgent need to further orient ourselves towards providing quality services to both our external and internal customers to their entire satisfaction/expectations. Keeping this in mind, a separate factor on 'Customer Orientation' has been included in the appraisal form. Internal customer in this factor denotes work/quality/service being provided by one department to another internally, example materials department supplies appropriate quality material to the production department and as such production department that in turn should satisfy the needs/expectations of the production department

VARIANCE & CONTRADICTIONS IN THE APPRAISAL

If the appraiser do not spend enough time before the appraisal discussion then there are chances of contradictions & variance emerging on the topics like the ratings of job performance, personal qualities, strong & weak points, growth potential and training needs etc.

There is a common thread linking the various constituents of the appraisal system and as such, there has to be proper collaboration between the rating and comments in the various constituents as mentioned above.

ROLE OF THE HEAD OF THE DEPARTMENT

The Department. Head should finalize the appraisal form on the basis of his personal knowledge of the appraises performance, strong points/week points, potential for growth & training needs etc. While finalizing, the Head also reviews the appraisal done by the Immediate Superior and the remarks about guidelines/system check by HRD.

Encourage proper standards of evaluation in your Department.

Conduct the appraisal discussion in a smooth and healthy manner and find objectives and targets for the next year.

Decide what 'Follow-up Actions' i.e. training, transfer, job rotation, job enrichment is to be imparted, alongwith the HRD.

Assess the growth potential of the appraise. The level & type of work in near future i.e. in 1 to 2 years & in distant future i.e. more than 2 years.

ROLE OF HRD

The success of the appraisal system in an Organization will depend on the role played by HRD in implementing and monitoring the system.

The HRD Department. should explain the concept, appraisal guidelines and implementation procedure and carry out the necessary training and counseling, wherever required.

It is very important that the appraisal forms are completed timely and objectively and that each form is scrutinized by the HRD Department. for proper filling up of the forms as per the system and guidelines before the Appraisal Interview takes place.

During the Appraisal Discussion a representative from HRD Department. acting as an observer should be present..

APPRAISAL DISCUSSION

One of the most important aspect of a good appraisal system is conducting of the proper Appraisal Discussion with the appraise.

For this, the Head of the department has to allot sufficient time to both appraiser and appraise. He should also to make sure that the Appraisal Discussion ends with a proper understanding between the appraiser and appraise.

Now question is how to conduct the Appraisal Discussion?

The Appraisal Discussion should start with the job description to avoid ambiguity, if any. The appraiser should convey the idea - " All of us have strengths and weaknesses". Then enlist the strong points/ accomplishment of objectives with incidents and examples.

The weak points should be taken up also.

Training Needs and Growth Potential should be discussed and made sure that it is taken positively by the appraise.

During the Appraisal Discussion objectives and targets set in the previous year should be discussed and analyzed that how much has been achieved. A format for objectives and targets has been prepared. Also set objectives and targets for the next year. Joint action plans should be formulated for improving the weaknesses and building over strengths.

The signature of the "Appraise" is to acknowledge that the Appraisal Discussion took place. It does not mean that the appraise agrees or does not agree with the entire appraisal.

If the Appraise does not accept a particular rating in spite of detailed discussion with examples etc. then the same may be briefly recorded in the given column.

Table 16

SONALIKA OBJECTIVES AND TARGETS SHEET

Mutually set by employee and his superior FROM

Name: Employee code:

Designation:

Unit:

Performance Area	ACTIVITY	Expected Results Time frame

Signature of Employee

Signature of Manager Superior

Date:

Date:

FOLLOW UP ACTIONS

Training needs should clearly emerge from the appraisal system for covering weaknesses and for development and growth of the individual.

Follow up actions regarding job rotation, job enrichment, transfer and career pathing should be recorded on the appraisal form at the end and implemented jointly by the Departmental Head and HRD.

For the proper implementation, it is desirable that HRD maintains a register showing the follow-up actions recorded from the appraisal form of each individual employee. It should monitor the progess regularly.

Table 17

SONALIKA PERFORMANCE APPRAISAL FORM

Unit:

Review Period:

From ____________________ To ____________________

Rating Key

(A) Performance exceptionally higher than the requirement of the job.

(B) Performance consistently exceeds the requirement of the job.

(C) Performance meets the requirement of the job.

(D) Performance needs improvement to meet the requirement of the job.

Personal Data

Name:

S.C No:

Qualification

DOJ:

Department:

Experience before joining: ________ Years.

Designation and Grade on joining:

Present Designation and Grade:

Training Programs attended in last two years:

Job Description: (To be filled by Immediate Superior)

Previous:

Present (Since When?)

(To be filled by Appraisee and signed by head of department with his remarks)

Objectives & Targets of last year

Your Accomplishments with regard to the Objectives & targets and the result thereon.

Personal Traits/Skills:

Factors Narrative Assessment

Rating - A,B,C,D

(Reason. Information. Data. Incident supporting the rating.)

LEADERSHIP

(Ability to motivate lead and guide his team in achieving the objectives

PLANNING & ORGANISING

Methodical sequence of work in advance as per Priorities, allocating work and monitoring result

COMMUNICATION

(Communication clear and precise both verbal and written e.g. in instructions, discussions, reports letters etc.)

OPENNESS

(Participative transparent dealing encourages feedback & criticism builds trust and faith)

TEAM WORK

(Participates as team member encourages supportive and committed efforts of the individuals in achieving the common objectives within his area and across the function)

ORGANISATIONAL APPROACH

(Takes into account Organizational interest and works purposefully towards the achievement of its objectives.)

DELEGATION & SUBORDIANTE DEVELOPMENT

(Training & Developing subordinates and passing down responsible work for effective working)

JUDGEMENT & DECISION MAKING

(Diagnosing the problem/situation in its elements and selecting aptly in time the best course out of available alternatives)

INITIATIVE

(Proactive, anticipates situations and takes action in time.)

ATTITUDE AND CONDUCT:

(Committed to work, has positive behavior, willing, cooperative and follows company rules & regulations)

MATURITY

(Studies situations in depth and totality, considers other's viewpoint, has balanced opinion. Remains calm under stress.)

MANNERS AND GENERAL BEARING

(Dress, personal appearance and habits)

JOB KNOWLEDGE

(Knowledge of one's job including theoretical and practical aspects)

EFFICIENCY AND PRODUCTIVITY

(Maximum quality output with minimum inputs like time, material, equipment and cost.

QUALITATIVE AND QUANTITATIVE OUTPUT

(Consistently accurate work as per standards, quality of work in relation to expected output.)

CROSS FUNCTIONAL KNOWLEDGE

(Working knowledge of other related functions and activities in the organization)

CONTINUOUS CHANGE AND IMPROVEMENT

(Receptive, brings change and improvement in work, quality process and behavior.

CUSTOMER ORIENTATION (Keeps needs and expectations of the external and An internal customer in mind while performing tasks.

Any other Point

- ☆ Summary

- ☆ Strong Points

- ☆ Weak Points

Growth Potential

In near future (1-2 years)

In long run (more than 2 Years)

Training requirements

(To overcome the weaker points and future development in job)

Appraisal Discussions with Appraisee

Present: 1. Immediate supervisor

2. Head of the Deptt.

3. H.R.D. Personnel

Signature Appraisee Signature Deptt Head

(Remarks: strong Points, Weak Points, Growth Potential or raining needs)

Follow up actions:

(Required for Job enrichment and enlargement, transfer, promotion, training, career planning etc)

Signature (Department Head) with date:

Signature (H.R.D) with date:

8
CONCLUSIONS

Personal records have always been very important and necessary for good personnel administration. As business continue to grow and the administration of personnel becomes more sophisticated and professional. The volume of records increases in proportion with the new technologies creating new and vastly different records.

Only sound records management can provide accurate information to organization with the necessary checks and balances in paper work and facilitate the retention of information in a uniform and specified manner. Good forms are created to save time and cost and to retain information in an orderly manner. So the main function of HR specialists is to maintain control over the operations and to keep a record of how effectively the human resources have been utilized.

The main functions of a record management program are:

- ☆ Record Creation
- ☆ Record Maintenance
- ☆ Record Disposal and
- ☆ Information Flow

The process of record creation involves the process of storing of data in man or machine in readable form. Record maintenance provides the means for controlling, analyzing, classifying and retrieving active recorded information. Record disposition provides the systematic removal of semi active records from expensive space, and concentrating on protection of active, vital and important records. Information flow helps to pass on the required information or data at appropriate time for further decision.

The company International Tractors Limited, engaged in manufacturing agricultural equipments under the trademark of SONALIKA. A small factory was established in seventies at Hoshiarpur in Punjab. This factory, which produced only fifty machines in the year of establishment, started producing five thousand units within few years and at present it is producing seventy five thousand units per year. A new facility equipped with "state of the art" modern machinery has already become operative covering an area of fifteen thousand square meters. So is the staff. At present there are more than two thousand workers on the pay roll. But the system of keeping a personnel records of all the employees in a uniform system was not undertaken that way, which requires a through management skill.

The existing personnel record system has some shortcomings. There is no standard form available to inform the personnel department, about the need for manpower in the department. This information is communicated though memos and letters to the personnel department.

The curriculum vitae of candidates desirous of employment in SONALIKA are voluminous and are maintained according to their qualifications in various files. Forms of candidates who are found unfit by the organization are also maintained in the same files. However, it is very difficult to access relevant information from these files. There is alternate system of storage of information.

There exists no means of ensuring that the personnel have imparted all the information that is required by a new inductee. There is also no means of judging the efficacy of the induction programme for the new inductee.

The training need of the employee is highlighted by the annual performance appraisal. However there in no means for the personnel department to capture information needed by it to tackle the training needs of individuals, which are highlighted during other periods of time. A standard form to capture such data would go long way to help the personnel to consolidate this data and to take action subsequently on these training needs.

However the personnel department maintains personal records of employees, but there is no consolidation of information available in the personnel files of the individual. There is no means available to elicit employee suggestions about improvements in their work

The personnel department is required to send certain information to the corporate office at the end of every week. The information heads are specified. However there is no standard way of presentation of this information in a clear and standard manner.

So keeping these shortcomings in mind various new forms have been designed and old are modified to co-op with the changing scenario and needs of the company. Basically Sonalika is a family business concern headed by family members. Keeping in view the growth of the company, the speed of developmental change in the information system is slow. Information is centered in the hands of top management. Flow of information is slightly one way i.e. from top to bottom. Now company is working on decentralization of decision-making powers. New professionally qualified personnel have been inducted to steam line the system on international standards.

BIBLIOGRAPHY

BOOKS

Davar, Rustom S. Personnel Management and Industrial Relations in India (New Delhi: Vikas Publishing House Pvt. Limited 1976)

Gupta, Ashok Kumar, Emerging Pattern of Political Leadership, (New Delhi; Mittal Publications, 1991)

Decenzo, David A. & Robbins Stephen P. Personnel/ Human Resource Management (New Delhi: Prentice Hall of India Pvt. Limited, 1993)

Flippo, Edwin B. Personnel Management (New York: McGraw Hill Book Co., 1984)

Famularo, Joseph J. ed. Handbook of modern Personnel Administration (New York: Mc Graw Hill Book Co., 1972)

Gupta, Ashok Kumar, Developing Human Resource Information System in an growing organization special reference to International Tractors Limited, a dissertation submitted to School of Management Studies (SOMS), Indira Gandhi National Open University (IGNOU), New Delhi 2002

Jucius, Michael J. Personnel Management (Illinois: Richard D. Irwin Inc., 1955)

Young, Pauline V. Scientific Social Surveys and Research (New Delhi: Prentice Hall of India Pvt. Limited, 1982)

Students Reading Material, School of Management Studies (SOMS), Indira Gandhi National Open University (IGNOU), (relevant chapters).

PERIODICALS

The Hindu, New Delhi

Times of India, New Delhi.

Hindustan Times, New Delhi.

The Economic Times, New Delhi.

Business Today.

Economic and Political weekly

India Today.

Various Reports of Sonalika Group of companies

WEB SITES

Lots of websites visited apart from company's website